BAT CITIZENS

Defending the Ninjas of the Night

by ROB LAIDLAW

First published in Canada and the United States in 2018

www.pajamapress.ca   info@pajamapress.ca

The publisher gratefully acknowledges the support of the Canada Council for the
Arts and the Ontario Arts Council for its publishing program. We acknowledge the
financial support of the Government of Canada through the Canada Book Fund
(CBF) for our publishing activities.

Library and Archives Canada Cataloguing in Publication

Laidlaw, Rob, author   **Bat citizens : defending the ninjas of the night /**
Rob Laidlaw.

Includes index.
ISBN 978-1-77278-039-0 (hardcover)

    1. Bats--Juvenile literature. I. Title.

QL737.C5L25 2018   j599.4   C2017-906553-X

Publisher Cataloging-in-Publication Data (U.S.)

Names: Laidlaw, Rob, 1959-, author.
Title: Bat Citizens : Defending the Ninjas of the Night / Rob Laidlaw.
Description: Toronto, Ontario Canada : Pajama Press, 2018. | Includes index. |
Summary: "An informational book about bats' biology, history, habitats, and the
environmental challenges they face. 'Bat Citizen' profiles highlight the work of
young conservationists. Includes full-color photographs throughout, along with a
table of contents, index, glossary, sidebars, and center gatefold bat illustration"—
Provided by publisher.
Identifiers: ISBN 978-1-77278-039-0 (hardcover)
Subjects: LCSH: Bats – Juvenile literature. | Bats – Conservation-- Juvenile lit-
erature. | BISAC: JUVENILE NONFICTION / Animals / Animal Welfare. |
JUVENILE NONFICTION / Animals / Nocturnal.
Classification: LCC QL737.C5L353 |DDC 599.4 – dc23
Gatefold illustration by Barry Kent MacKay
Cover Image: Jamaican fruit bat flying at night–
Shutterstock/©BlueRingMedia; silhouettes– Shutterstock/©Anastasiia Sorokina
Cover and book design by Lorena Gonzalez Guillen

Manufactured by Qualibre Inc./Print Plus
Printed in China

Pajama Press Inc.
181 Carlaw Ave. Suite 207 Toronto, Ontario Canada, M4M 2S1
Distributed in Canada by UTP Distribution
5201 Dufferin Street Toronto, Ontario Canada, M3H 5T8

Distributed in the U.S. by Ingram Publisher Services
1 Ingram Blvd. La Vergne, TN 37086, USA

BAT CITIZENS
Defending the Ninjas of the Night
ROB LAIDLAW

Dedicated to the memory of
Heather MacEwan Foran,
a passionate and tireless
advocate for all animals

CONTENTS

INTRODUCTION

The first time I saw bats was on a warm summer evening in Ontario, Canada. I could spot several of them darting in and out of the beam of a streetlight, catching moths. That's probably the way most people encounter bats.

Since that time, I've encountered bats around the world in towns and cities, wilderness parks and reserves, and underground in caves and mines. I've observed captive bats in wildlife rescue centers, zoos, and even kept as pets. I've learned how complex, intelligent, and social bats are; why they are critically important to natural ecosystems; and how beneficial bats are to humans. I've also discovered that bats are in trouble and need our help. Bats are disappearing because of threats like habitat destruction, roost disturbance, disease, and wind turbines.

But there is hope for bats. Throughout the world, people are working on their behalf. The young people I profile in this book—I call them Bat Citizens—show that anyone can help bats. I hope this book changes the way you think about bats and inspires you to get active helping them. I'm confident that if enough of us get involved, bats will be with us for many years to come.

—ROB

Did you know that over 20% of all the mammal species in the world are bats?

Bat Squad! is Bat Conservation International's webcast series made for kids by kids. They spread the word about bat conservation and research through free online broadcasts during BCI's annual Bat Week. Watch for their logo throughout this book to see which of our Bat Citizens are involved.

MANY KINDS OF BATS

More than 1,300 species of bats have been identified, and new species are discovered from time to time. Bats range in size from the Kitti's hog-nosed bat (*Craseonycteris thonglong-yai*), also called the bumblebee bat, just 1.25 inches long (30 millimeters) and weighing only as much as a dime, to the largest flying foxes, like the giant golden-crowned flying fox (*Acerodon jubatus*), which has a wingspan of 6.6 feet (2 meters) and a weight of about 2 pounds (1 kilogram).

Most bats are brownish or dark in color, but there are striped, patterned, and white bats too. Bat coloration is usually an adaptation that hides them from predators. Dark colors blend in with tree bark, rocks, and shadowy recesses. Striped, mottled, or white bats blend in with the dappled sunlight in vegetation, especially when viewed from below. Two of the most beautiful kinds of bats are butterfly bats (*Glauconycteris variegata*) and painted bats (*Kerivoula picta*).

While bats share many common features, they also have great diversity, including different kinds of faces, ears, teeth, tongues, thumbs, feet, claws, and tails.

A beautiful butterfly bat

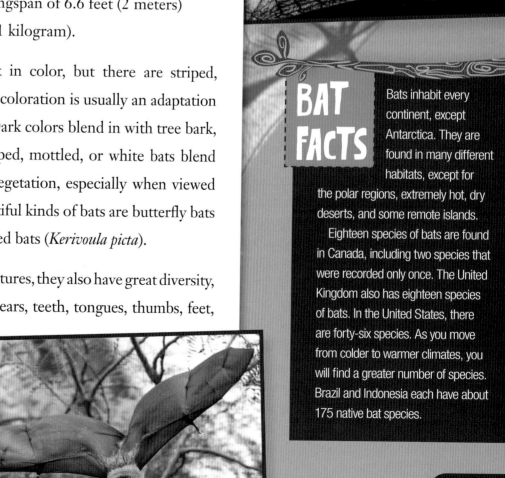

A giant golden-crowned flying fox

BAT FACTS

Bats inhabit every continent, except Antarctica. They are found in many different habitats, except for the polar regions, extremely hot, dry deserts, and some remote islands.

Eighteen species of bats are found in Canada, including two species that were recorded only once. The United Kingdom also has eighteen species of bats. In the United States, there are forty-six species. As you move from colder to warmer climates, you will find a greater number of species. Brazil and Indonesia each have about 175 native bat species.

Many species capture returning echoes with specially adapted facial features and large ears

WHAT IS ECHOLOCATION?

Microbats produce high-frequency sounds in their larynx (part of their throat) and then emit them in pulses through their mouth or nose. The sounds bounce off objects, and the bats listen to the returning echoes and interpret them. Echolocation allows bats to map the area around them, avoid colliding with objects, and find potential prey in total darkness.

Echolocation is mostly used over short distances, somewhere between 16–65 feet (5–20 meters). All microbats use echolocation but only three megabats do, and the sounds *they* produce come from clicking their tongues.

Bats also make other sounds to communicate with each other. Mothers may use sound to locate their pups. The squeaks of Egyptian fruit bats may be arguments over food or sleeping position, or how another bat is getting too close. Male bats of some species sing or have special calls to attract mates. Many bats use alarm calls to alert others of danger.

WHAT EXACTLY ARE BATS?

Bats are warm-blooded mammals. They have hair on their bodies, and the females nurse their young with milk from mammary glands. They are scientifically classified in the order Chiroptera, a Greek term that means "hand wing." Bats are *not* closely related to rodents or birds. Today, some scientists believe bats are more closely related to shrews, flying lemurs, or primates, or to a superorder (a category of related animals) called Laurasiatheria, which includes carnivores and whales and dolphins.

The order Chiroptera is divided into two major categories, called suborders. One is Megachiroptera (megabats), with approximately 200 species of Old World fruit bats and flying foxes. The other category is Microchiroptera (microbats), with an estimated 1,100 species of primarily insectivorous (insect-eating) bats that use echolocation.

The terms are not perfect. Some microbats are bigger than some megabats, and some megabats use a primitive form of echolocation. And new suborders are now recognized, the Yinpterochiroptera (comprised of megabats and five microbat families) and the Yangochiroptera (all the other microbats). However, to keep things simple in this book I use the terms megabats and microbats.

The Egyptian fruit bat uses a form of echolocation

Bats may be related to shrews (top) or flying lemurs (bottom)

BAT CITIZEN: TRUTH MULLER
BUDDIES FOR BATS

Truth Muller, from Rock Hill, New York, always thought bats were cool animals. When he was eleven years old, a government biologist informed Truth that a new disease, called white-nose syndrome, had killed 93% of the bats in his area. Truth started Buddies for Bats to inform people about the disease and about why bats are so environmentally important. Truth started with just a small display and has since reached more than three million people, raising awareness about bats through his presentations at schools, libraries, fairs, and special events throughout the state. Newspaper, radio, and television stories have increased Truth's reach even further. Buddies for Bats also supports other efforts to help bats, including lobbying for endangered status for the northern long-eared bat. Truth has won awards for his excellent work on behalf of bats and has become the youngest ever member of Bat Conservation International's Speakers Bureau.

Honduran white bats create their own shelters out of leaves

WHICH ROOST?

Maternity roosts are where female bats gather to bear their young. Their combined body heat may help create a warm environment for the helpless pups.

Hibernacula are winter hibernation roosts. During winter, bats need stable, cool temperatures that do not change very much, and moist air that helps reduce the loss of body fluids.

A roosting Indiana bat

SAFE HAVENS FOR BATS

Bats are found in cities, towns, farmland, open grassland, forests, mountains, and deserts. Wherever they are found they look for roosts (a place where they can rest during the day) that will protect them from predators and provide comfortable sleeping conditions. Particularly good roosts may be used for decades or more.

Bats can roost underneath bridges and in caves, mines, subterranean crevices, tunnels, wells, and culverts. They can also roost in attics, basements, barns, abandoned buildings, and church towers. Other bats roost in dense foliage, tree cavities, burrows, hollow bamboo shoots, termite mounds, or under loose tree bark or rocks. Tent-making bats create their own shelters by biting along the middle rib of a leaf and then folding it over so they can hang underneath.

Some bats have many roosts, moving from one to another regularly. Some change roosts according to season, food availability, or because their roosts have been disturbed. Depending on the species, bats may live alone, in small colonies, or in the millions.

Some bats migrate hundreds of miles or more to maternity or hibernation roosts, or they migrate seasonally to areas where food is available.

A colony of Virginia big-eared bats

Non-hibernating bats often fly south to warmer areas when cold weather arrives, but bats that hibernate may fly in any direction to get to their preferred hibernation roosts.

Bats may abandon their roosts if they are disturbed or if the habitat around them is destroyed. Often, changes made by humans force bats to find new roosts that may not be as good as the old ones.

BAT CITIZEN: DARA MCANULTY
MAKING A BAT-FRIENDLY WORLD

In Northern Ireland, thirteen-year-old conservationist Dara McAnulty does whatever he can to help bats and other wild animals. Dara blogs about bats, his own wildlife sightings and research, and his thoughts about wildlife conservation. He constructs bat boxes for local gardens, schools, and other organizations. He also goes out with a local bat group to do bat detecting, and he contributes his findings to a database that helps scientists studying bats. Dara's dad holds a license to rescue bats, so Dara has learned a lot about bat rehabilitation and has participated in a number of successful bat releases. Through his writing and other activities, Dara wants to help build a community of people who love, respect, and care for all wildlife and the environments in which they live.

Batty Ideas

A BOX FULL OF BATS

The bat box idea is simple. Many small insectivorous bats like to roost in small, tight spaces as narrow as ½ inch (1.25 centimeters). Bat boxes are snug spaces where bats can roost comfortably. A bat box consists of one or more narrow slots (or chambers) with an open entrance at the bottom (unlike birdhouses, which have a side entry hole and a floor). The bats enter from the bottom, squeeze inside, and hang by their feet. The boxes should be hung 13 feet (4 meters) or more above the ground in a place predators will find hard to reach. They should also receive as much sunlight as possible because bats need the warmth, especially if there are pups inside. Painting the box black helps because black absorbs sunlight. Depending on its size, a bat box can house anywhere from just a few bats to many hundreds or thousands. There are lots of free bat box designs on the internet.

Dara McAnulty

A bat house seen from below

A NATURAL WONDER UNLIKE ANY OTHER

Just before dusk, I watched a small stream of bats start to emerge from Bracken Cave near San Antonio, Texas. Their numbers quickly rose to hundreds and then thousands until a massive tornado-like spiral of Mexican free-tailed bats (*Tadarida brasiliensis mexicana*) rose up from the cave. The bats then flew off in a twisting, turning, snake-like ribbon that stretched as far as the eye could see. I had never seen anything like it.

Weighing less than a quarter, Mexican free-tailed bats are incredibly powerful flyers. Some travel 60 miles (100 kilometers) or more to forage for insects and then fly all the way back in the morning. They face many hazards along the way, including predators, and some of them don't make it back. I watched a red-tailed hawk flying into the ribbon of bats and snatching them out of the air one at a time.

After ninety minutes of watching, I had to leave. The bats were still exploding out of the cave and would keep coming for hours yet. Not surprising since there were an estimated 20 million bats in the cave. I left knowing I had observed one of the great wildlife spectacles of the world.

Free-tailed bats have tails that extend beyond the uropatagium, a membrane that stretches between a bat's legs

Bracken Cave entrance

BRACKEN CAVE SAVED

Because Bracken Cave is just 20 miles (32 kilometers) from the city of San Antonio, Texas, urban development has put the cave at risk. To protect the bats, The Nature Conservancy (TNC) and Bat Conservation International (BCI) purchased Bracken Cave and the property around it. The owners of some neighboring properties also entered into a conservation easement (a voluntary agreement that ensured their properties would not be developed or changed in ways that could harm the bats). It seemed as though the future of Bracken Cave and of the bats was secure.

But then BCI found out about a plan to construct 3,500 homes on a piece of land just south of Bracken Cave and right underneath the bats' nightly flight path. The development could be very disruptive to the bats. There was no legal way to stop the project, so BCI started an awareness campaign about the threat. Thousands of people spoke out in favor of protecting the bats. News stories about Bracken Cave appeared in Texas and across the country. Local politicians took notice and joined the effort.

In the end, the land developers, the city, and the conservation groups reached a deal. The groups ended up buying the land for $20.5 million. Once again, the bats were safe.

This Mexican free-tailed bat's wing membrane will probably heal itself after being pierced on a cactus spine

A BCI staff member with her bat assistant

Visitors of all ages watch bats emerge from Bracken Cave

A bat's wing under ultraviolet light

BAT CITIZEN: SARAH GORTON
HOOKED ON BATS

At thirteen years old, Sarah Gorton started volunteering at a local zoo and fell in love with bats. She became a zoo docent (somebody who teaches zoo visitors) at sixteen and then an intern for its teen program. After receiving her rabies vaccination, Sarah started to help out at a local wildlife rehabilitation center and volunteered at nearby Bracken Cave. During one of her spring breaks, Sarah drove for two days to spend a week with the Missouri Bat Census. She surveyed several caves and learned how to humanely trap bats and use ultraviolet light to check their wings for signs of white-nose syndrome.

Sarah's next trip was to Georgia, where she spent three months assisting with bat research. Today, Sarah is running her own bat research projects, including two that involve acoustic monitoring, one creating bat-focused lesson plans for teachers, and one looking at how the news media portrays bats. Now nineteen years old, Sarah continues to be hooked on bats and will continue to do everything she can to help them.

CRISPY, CRUNCHY, SLIMY, TASTY

Most microbats eat flying insects such as moths, beetles, mosquitos, and dragonflies. While in flight, the bats grab the insects with their sharp teeth or by using their wing or tail membranes like a net to scoop them up. Remarkably, many bats can consume up to their own weight in insects every night. Females with pups can eat even more.

There are also microbats that hunt by sight and sound for ground-dwelling spiders, worms, slugs, and insects like cicadas, katydids, grasshoppers, and termites. Carnivorous microbats hunt for frogs, lizards, birds, small mammals, and other bats. Some even eat fish. There are also bats that consume nothing but blood.

BAT FACTS

ESCAPE ARTISTS

Many flying insects have developed features and evasive behaviors that help them deal with bat attacks. For example, when moths with bat-detecting ears hear bat echolocation signals, they respond by flying rapidly and erratically or dropping straight down into the nearest clump of vegetation to hide. A few moths send out sounds that are believed to briefly interrupt bat signals, giving the moths a chance to escape.

Some tiger moths may use sound to confuse and escape bats

Fruit bat teeth are made to pierce tough fruit skins

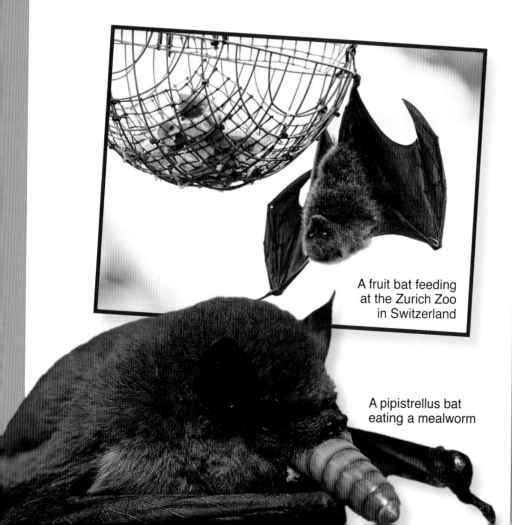

A fruit bat feeding at the Zurich Zoo in Switzerland

A pipistrellus bat eating a mealworm

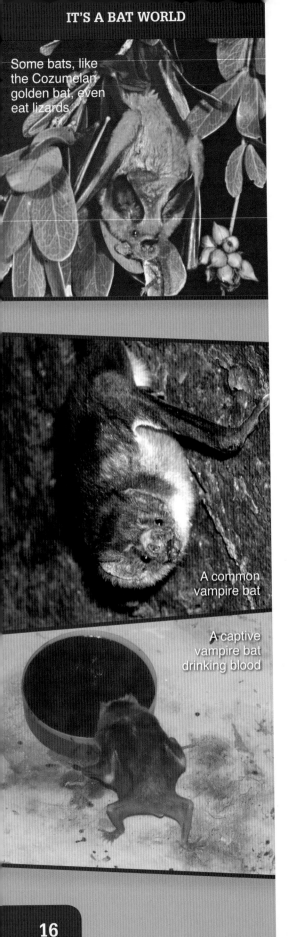

Some bats, like the Cozumelan golden bat, even eat lizards

A common vampire bat

A captive vampire bat drinking blood

FISHING BATS

Six bat species, including the fish-eating myotis (*Myotis vivesi*), consume fish. Using echolocation, the bats detect surface disturbances on the water. Then they fly just above the surface, dragging their long legs and big-clawed feet through the water until they grab a fish. The fish is then eaten eaten in flight or taken to a perch.

VAMPIRES DO EXIST!

There are only three species of sanguinivorous, or blood-eating, bats: the common vampire bat (*Desmodus rotundus*), the hairy-legged vampire bat (*Diphylla ecaudata*), and the white-winged vampire bat (*Diaemus youngi*). All are found in Central and South America. With their sharp teeth, they scoop out a tiny piece of their prey's skin and then lick blood from the wound. A chemical in their saliva keeps the blood flowing, but they drink only a tiny amount—less than 1 ounce (28 grams) per night.

The hairy-legged vampire bat roosts in very small colonies

SUCCULENT, SWEET NECTAR AND FRUIT

The frugivorous, or fruit-eating, bats have teeth adapted for biting through hard fruit skins and for crushing fruit. Since food moves so rapidly through their digestive systems before being eliminated, many of the fruit seeds are left intact. For that reason, fruit bats are the most important seed dispersers in tropical forests.

Nectarivorous bats that feed on nectar and pollen are important pollinators for hundreds of plant species. When they insert their long tongues (some with bushy tips) and snouts into flowers to drink nectar, pollen is picked up. When they go to other flowers, the pollen is transferred. They are the nighttime equivalent of daytime pollinators, like hummingbirds and bees.

Some plants are adapted to attract bats. They produce showy light-colored flowers, strong smells, lots of nectar, and night-blooming flowers. Nectar-eating bats are more common in Africa, Southeast Asia, and the Pacific, but they are also found in North and South America.

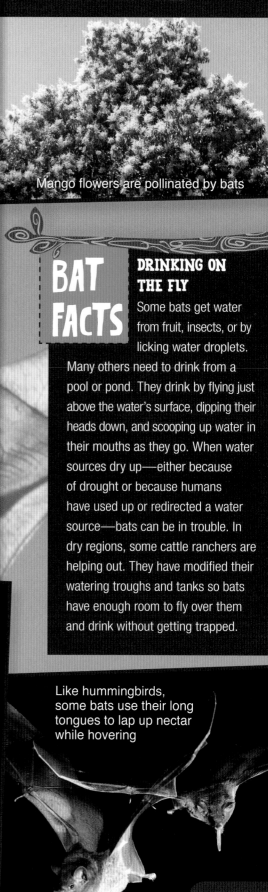

Mango flowers are pollinated by bats

BAT FACTS

DRINKING ON THE FLY

Some bats get water from fruit, insects, or by licking water droplets. Many others need to drink from a pool or pond. They drink by flying just above the water's surface, dipping their heads down, and scooping up water in their mouths as they go. When water sources dry up—either because of drought or because humans have used up or redirected a water source—bats can be in trouble. In dry regions, some cattle ranchers are helping out. They have modified their watering troughs and tanks so bats have enough room to fly over them and drink without getting trapped.

A leaf-nosed bat coming in for a drink

A grey-headed flying fox feeding on nectar

Like hummingbirds, some bats use their long tongues to lap up nectar while hovering

17

UNBELIEVABLE BAT BIOLOGY!

Batty Ideas

BAT BEGINNINGS

The earliest bat fossil is from the Eocene Epoch, approximately 52 million years ago, and it looks a lot like a modern microbat. The earliest fossil remains of a megabat, however, appeared much later—about 35 million years ago. Many scientists believe the early ancestors of bats might have been small gliding mammals—like today's flying squirrels—that gradually evolved moveable wings and the ability to fly.

Compared to other small animals, bats live a very long time

SENIOR CITIZEN BATS

Small mammals tend to have short lifespans, while big mammals tend to have long lifespans. Bats are an exception to that rule and can live from about eight to forty years or more. One little brown bat (*Myotis lucifugus*) in Ontario, Canada, was documented at thirty-one years old, but the oldest known bat in the wild was a Brandt's myotis (*Myotis brandtii*) in Siberia that was at least forty-four years old. More than twenty different bat species are known to live longer than twenty years, and at least five species are known to live longer than thirty years in the wild. The microbats that hibernate for months each year seem to live the longest of all. However, some of the non-hibernating flying foxes have survived for twenty-five years or more in zoos. In addition to flight and echolocation, the exceptionally long lifespans of bats make them different from all other small mammals.

This captive fruit bat could live for more than 20 years

BAT CITIZEN: OSCAR SCHOLIN
TEAM CHIROPTERA

In the seventh grade, Oscar Scholin joined Team Chiroptera, a new Pacific Grove Middle School club that would be studying bats in the Monterey Bay area of California. As a lifelong lover of bats, Oscar jumped at the opportunity. With some expert help, Oscar and the team devised a research project to find out if bat activity was different depending on the size of their habitat in the Monterey pine ranges. They placed audio recorders in 19 pine ranges and collected 4,300 bat calls. Surprisingly, they found the size of the habitat didn't seem to make much difference to bat activity levels. However, the team thought they might have needed additional recorders in the larger habitats as some bat calls may have been missed. Their research led to a poster presentation at the 2015 symposium of the North American Society for Bat Research. Since that time, Oscar and the team have been out with handheld bat detectors, trying to determine where local bats prefer to roost and forage.

BAT FACTS

ACOUSTIC BAT DETECTORS

Since many bat sounds are ultrasonic (too high for humans to hear), researchers and bat enthusiasts use acoustic bat detectors to locate bats and listen to them. These devices can either play the sounds back at a pitch humans can hear or record the sound as digital information that can be studied on a computer.

Oscar Scholin using an acoustic bat detector

19

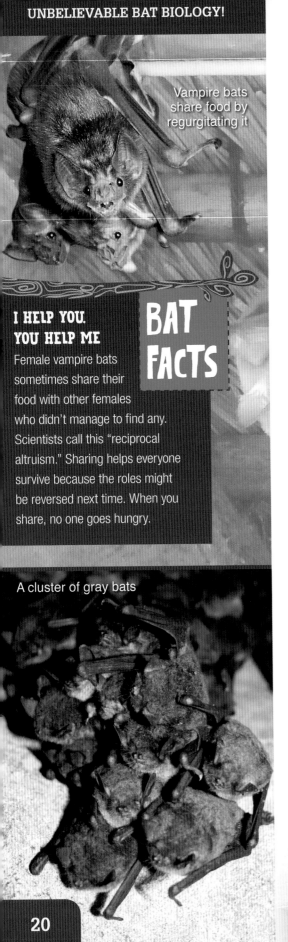

Vampire bats share food by regurgitating it

I HELP YOU. YOU HELP ME

BAT FACTS

Female vampire bats sometimes share their food with other females who didn't manage to find any. Scientists call this "reciprocal altruism." Sharing helps everyone survive because the roles might be reversed next time. When you share, no one goes hungry.

A cluster of gray bats

A LONG, DEEP SLEEP

Hibernation allows bats to survive cold periods when food isn't available. Bats store up fat reserves in their bodies to get ready for a deep sleep. When they enter hibernation, their body temperature drops and body processes, such as heart rate and breathing, slow down drastically. An active microbat's heart rate can be more than 1,000 beats per minute, but during hibernation it can drop to just 5 beats per minute. Bats may wake from hibernation several times to drink or relieve themselves, but if they wake up too often their fat stores will be used up and they won't survive.

BAT FAMILIES AND FRIENDS

Bats may live alone, in small clusters, or in large colonies. But all bats have social interactions with other bats and most live with or near them. Courtship and mating activities vary according to species. Bats that hibernate tend to mate in the fall, but pups aren't born until the next spring when the weather is better and insect food is available. In areas of year-round warm weather, courtship and breeding may occur at other times of the year. Births always take place at times when there is plenty of food.

Good hibernation conditions have attracted large numbers of gray bats

PRODUCING PUPS

While some bats have twins or multiple young, most female bats give birth to just one pup each year. The maternity season can vary around the world, but births usually occur from April to early June in North America.

Pups are huge at birth; they can weigh up to 30% of their mother's weight. To give birth, females turn head-upward, possibly because gravity helps with the birth in that position. If young females stay in an upside-down position, sometimes other females with more experience turn them around.

A newborn pup bonds with its mother while she licks it clean. The baby clings to her fur and, with her help, attaches itself to one of the nipples located near her armpits. That position allows the female to cover her helpless pup with a wing, keeping it safe and warm. When foraging (seeking food), some females leave their pups at the roost, coming back to check on them occasionally. Other mothers take their pups along.

Pups usually suckle (drink their mother's milk) for a month or two, but it can be longer for larger bats.

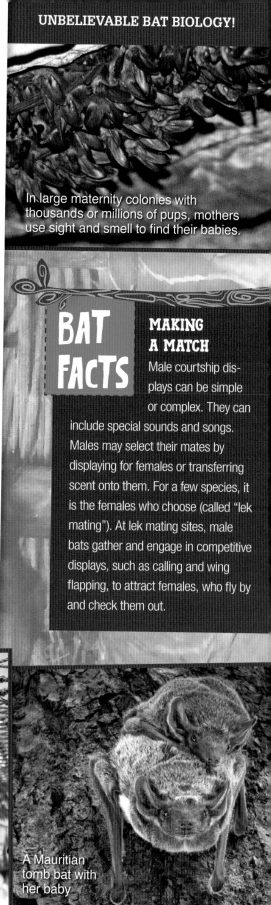

In large maternity colonies with thousands or millions of pups, mothers use sight and smell to find their babies.

BAT FACTS

MAKING A MATCH

Male courtship displays can be simple or complex. They can include special sounds and songs. Males may select their mates by displaying for females or transferring scent onto them. For a few species, it is the females who choose (called "lek mating"). At lek mating sites, male bats gather and engage in competitive displays, such as calling and wing flapping, to attract females, who fly by and check them out.

A spectacled flying fox and her pup (right)

A young Daubenton's bat

A Mauritian tomb bat with her baby

Batty Ideas

THE MISGUIDED WAR ON VAMPIRES

As the numbers of farm animals in Central and South America increase, so do the common vampire bats (*Desmodus rotundus*) that feed on their blood. An exaggerated fear of the bats spreading diseases, like rabies, to people and animals has led to the killing of millions of bats with a poison called vampiricide or, in some cases, with dynamite and flamethrowers. Unfortunately, many helpful pollinating and insect-eating bats have been killed too.

A civet

A mongoose

A coatimundi

NOT EVERYONE MAKES IT

Bats have many predators, including cats, dogs, snakes, weasels, skunks, raccoons, coatimundis, civets, mongooses, hawks, and owls, to name a few. The bat hawk from Africa and Asia and the bat falcon from Central and South America are specialized bat eaters. There is even a small songbird, the great tit, that was recently discovered preying on pipistrelle bats by pecking at them while they woke from hibernation.

Other bats may be predators too. The carnivorous spectral bat (*Vampyrum spectrum*) of Central and South America eats many small animals, including small bats.

Most bats don't survive beyond their first year. They face many dangers. Pups may fall from roosts. Inexperienced young bats might not find enough food or water, or they may fly into a fence or vehicle, be caught by predators, or get too close to a wind turbine.

The bat hawk's diet consists mostly of bats

A rat snake swallowing a bat

Most microbats have big **ears** to pick up returning echolocation signals

A bat's **elbow** helps it extend its wing

Hoary Bat

The wing **membrane** is stretchy and can heal itself if it tears

A bat's **wrist** is less flexible than that of other mammals

A bat's **nose** is very sensitive

Many microbats have tiny, sharp **teeth** for catching moths and other insects

BAT CITIZEN: LOGAN CARTER
SPREADING THE WORD ABOUT BATS

Lifelong animal lover Logan Carter has always been fascinated by bats. In fact, he never misses an opportunity to spread the word about how amazing bats are and why they need to be protected. Not only does Logan talk to friends, neighbors, and community members in his hometown of Muncie, Indiana, he also helps his bat biologist dad with the traveling Be a Bat Biologist exhibit. Even though Logan is only twelve years old, he's already educated thousands of children and adults about bats. In 2016, he became a member of Bat Conservation International's Bat Squad! and was featured in a four-part webcast series for schools across North America during Bat Week.

Batty Ideas

DEBUNKING BAT MYTHS

A common myth is that all bats carry diseases. In reality, most bats are healthy and disease free, and pose no threat whatsoever to humans. Unless someone handles a bat and is bitten, the chance of contracting a disease is almost zero. In fact, the disease risk posed by bats is less than the risk posed by many other animals, including dogs.

Another myth is that bats get caught in your hair. I've had hundreds of bats fly past me in caves, and I've never once had a bat make any contact at all. It's highly unlikely that a bat would ever be caught in someone's hair.

BATS ARE NOT BLIND!

There is no truth to the saying "blind as a bat." All bats can see. Echolocating microbats tend to have small eyes, while megabats have bigger eyes. Bats use sight for a lot of things, including orienting themselves, navigating during migration, and locating food such as fruit, flowers, and ground-dwelling prey.

WHO'S THE FASTEST IN THE SKIES?

Bats that fly high, fast, and far tend to have long, narrow wings. Bats with short, wide wings tend to fly slower but can change direction more quickly. Typical flying speeds are between 5 and 30 mph (8 and 50 kph). But it was recently discovered that Brazilian free-tailed bats fly as fast as 100 mph (160 kph), making them the world's fastest flying animals. They also fly extremely high, between 3,200 and 10,000 feet (1,000 to 3,000 meters).

BAT FACTS

NIGHT WINGS

While some other mammals can glide, only bats can fly. The wings of bats have a bone structure similar to human hands, with an upper arm, forearm, wrist, hand, and finger bones. Bats also have a thumb with a hooked claw. The long arm and finger bones provide support for a skin membrane that stretches to the bat's body. The hairless wing membrane is made of tough elastin (the protein that makes your skin stretchy) and muscle fibers. Many bats also have a membrane stretching between their legs and tail, called the *uropatagium*. It helps bats steer while flying, and it also helps them scoop up flying insects.

A Malayan flying fox

A Malayan flying fox wing

Hoary bats (*Lasiurus cinereus*) live in much of North and South America. With wingspans of up to 16 inches (40 centimeters), they are the largest bat in Canada. Their long, narrow wings make them strong and fast flyers, which is useful when they migrate long distances each year. They eat mostly moths and prefer to roost alone in trees. The hoary bat gets its name from white-tipped fur that makes it look frosted (*Hoarfrost* is another name for frost).

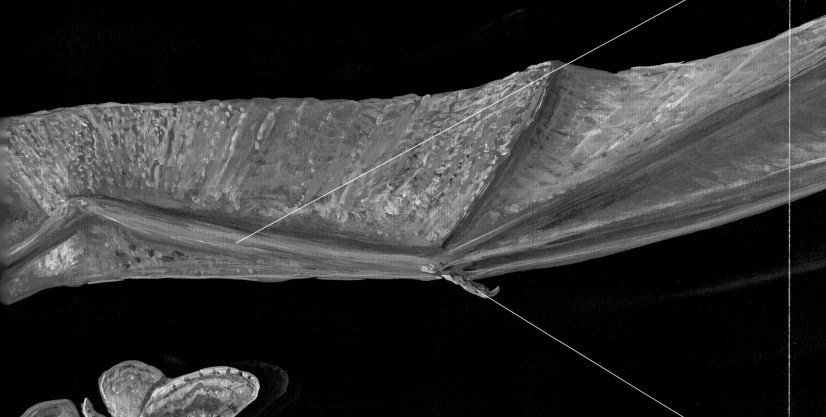

A bat's wing contains a
forearm and the same
types of bones as a human hand

A bat's wing bones are called
fingers

The claw-like hook on the
thumb is used
for climbing, holding onto food, and even fighting

Bats that use echolocation often have small **eyes**, but they are not blind

JUST HANGING AROUND

The leg bones of bats are long and relatively thin. Bats' legs can only support their full weight when they are hanging upside down. Specialized tendons in the toes of bats allow them to hang without using up any energy. The ability to hang upside down also allows bats to live in locations that predators can't access, like cave ceilings, and it gives them an easy way to escape: just let go and launch into flight. Some bats have a different way of hanging. The forest-dwelling disk-winged and sucker-footed bats have special suction disks on their ankles and wrists that allow them to cling to the smooth surfaces of leaves.

BAT FACTS

SPECIAL BAT POWERS

Bats' blood doesn't rush to their heads when they hang upside down. Special one-way valves in their arteries make sure blood that's pumped through their bodies can't flow backward.

Bats can also see what's behind them by using their extra-flexible necks to arch their heads all the way back.

The Malayan flying fox has sharp, curved claws

A lesser long-nosed bat pollinates a saguaro cactus flower.

Batty Ideas

PLANTING FORESTS

Fruit-eating bats are extremely important because they spread seeds from the fruits they eat, especially in tropical areas. Scientists believe that hundreds or possibly thousands of tree species are helped in this way. On some tropical islands, 25% or more of native trees may depend on bats for seed dispersal.

Bats may be our best allies in helping forests grow back in places where they have been cleared. Other seed dispersers, like monkeys or birds, avoid cleared areas. But bats will often fly right over, dropping seed-filled excrement as they go.

BATS FOR A HEALTHY WORLD

PREVENTING INSECT PLAGUES

Bats eat millions of tons of flying insects every year and help keep the number of pest insects under control. In the American Southwest, Mexican free-tailed bats (*Tadarida brasiliensis mexicana*) are the most important predators of corn borer moths. Without bats, farmers would have to spray more chemical pesticides on their crops, costing them more money and damaging the environment. Realizing how important bats' insect-control services are, many people are now trying to make agriculture more bat friendly.

POLLINATION POWERHOUSES

Hundreds of plant species, including the organ pipe and giant saguaro cactus in the United States, depend on bats for pollination. In fact, bat pollination (called chiropterophily) is essential to keeping some natural ecosystems healthy. A number of plant species would decrease or disappear if it were not for bats. Bats are also important to the economy because they pollinate a large number of commercially grown plants, such as mangoes, bananas, durian fruit, and agave.

BAT CITIZEN: CHRISTIAN SPAUR
HOMES FOR BATS

For as long as he can remember, Christian Spaur has been fascinated by bats. As a child he read every bat book he could find. When Christian was in elementary school his parents took him to a local bat census (a survey aimed at counting the number of species and individual bats in an area), where he saw wild bats up close for the first time. He learned how scientists netted the bats to collect information that would aid bat conservation.

When Christian was older and a member of the Boy Scouts, he focused on bats in his final project to earn the Eagle Scout designation, the highest achievement in the Boy Scouting program. Christian decided to install bat boxes in a wetland area on his local school's property. He notified the Ohio Division of Wildlife, spoke to his school superintendent, and obtained permission for the project from the school board by telling them about how beneficial bats are for mosquito control and the environment. The Ohio Division of Wildlife was so impressed with Christian that they kicked in some funding for the bat boxes and installation.

KEEP CALM and LOVE BATS

Mexican free-tailed bats

The "Nightwing" bat sculpture turns with the wind near the Congress Avenue Bridge

A BRIDGE FULL OF BATS

The Congress Avenue Bridge in Austin, Texas, was built in 1960 and overhauled in 1980. The repairs created tiny crevices between concrete slabs on the underside of the bridge. It wasn't long before Mexican free-tailed bats (*Tadarida brasiliensis mexicana*) started to move in. As their numbers grew, city health officials and local residents became concerned about disease. Local newspapers carried stories that exaggerated the disease risks, particularly of rabies, posed by the bats. Many residents were frightened and wanted the bats driven off or killed.

Then bat biologist Merlin Tuttle and his group, Bat Conservation International, stepped in and launched a campaign to save the bats. They informed residents and city officials that the bats were not a health hazard but were actually helpful and should be welcomed. They were successful and the city of Austin embraced the bats. Since that time, the bat population has grown to an estimated 1.5–2 million individuals.

CAUTION
You May Wish to Stand Back During Bat Flight, to Avoid Droppings

The Congress Avenue Bridge in Austin, Texas

BAT CITIZEN: RACHAEL BLOCK
BLOGGING FOR BATS

Fourteen-year-old Rachael Block's fascination with bats started when she watched a small colony of big brown bats (*Eptesicus fuscus*) roosting outside her house. In the sixth grade, Rachael read an article about local bat rehabilitator Leslie Sturges and decided to volunteer with her, but she soon discovered she wasn't old enough to do hands-on work. Instead, Leslie invited Rachael to write a regular blog for the Save Lucy Campaign, an organization she started to raise awareness about the disease white-nose syndrome (WNS). Rachael has been writing *Baturday News* ever since. Rachael also volunteers with Save Lucy at numerous events where she teaches children and adults about the importance of bats and how WNS is devastating bat populations. More recently, Rachael became a member of Bat Conservation International's Bat Squad!

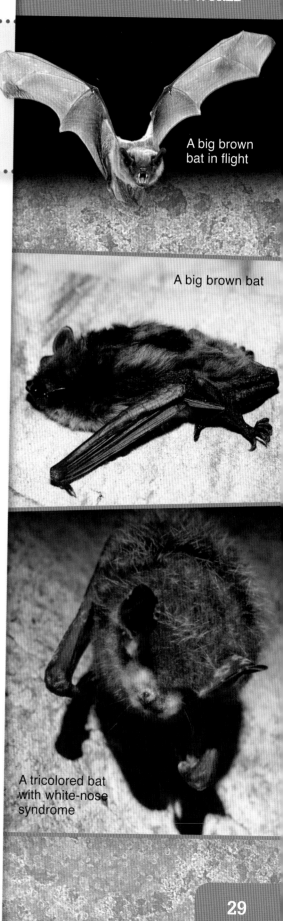

A big brown bat in flight

A big brown bat

A tricolored bat with white-nose syndrome

Rachael Block

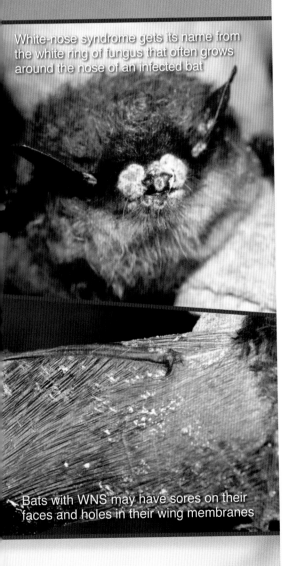

An estimated 7 million bats have already died because of WNS.

White-nose syndrome gets its name from the white ring of fungus that often grows around the nose of an infected bat

Bats with WNS may have sores on their faces and holes in their wing membranes

CHALLENGE: A DEADLY PLAGUE

In 2006, white-nose syndrome (WNS), a new disease affecting bats, was discovered in caves in New York State. By 2008, the disease had wiped out more than 90% of the caves' bat populations. Scientists soon realized that this new threat was the most serious one ever faced by bats in North America.

The white fungus, now known by the scientific name *Pseudogymnoascus destructans*, irritates hibernating bats, which causes them to wake up more often than normal and deplete or use up their fat reserves. When that happens, the bats leave their cave in search of food while it is still winter and then freeze or starve to death.

When I wrote this chapter, WNS was already in thirty-one U.S. states and five Canadian provinces. Bat-to-bat contact is the most likely way it spreads. But in March 2016, the first case of WNS was discovered in Washington State, 1,300 miles (2,092 kilometers) from the closest reported occurrence. Since the bats wouldn't have traveled that far, scientists believe the fungus may have been carried there on someone's clothes or shoes.

SOLUTION: HOPE IN THE WHITE-NOSE SYNDROME FIGHT

Together, scientists, conservation organizations, and governments are studying WNS to find ways of slowing or stopping its spread. One example of action being taken is the gating of caves, mines, tunnels, and other underground bat hibernation sites. If people are not allowed in, there is no chance they can help spread WNS to the bats inside. It's a good first step in the battle against WNS.

In 2016, the media reported that scientists at Georgia State University are working on a treatment to block the growth of the white-nose fungus, which might make the disease less severe. They are also working on a method of spraying the treatment into bat hibernacula.

There is reason for hope. A study conducted in Atlantic Canada showed that bat activity was up during the summer of 2015 in Prince Edward Island National Park. And some WNS-decimated bat populations seem to have stabilized on their own, although at about 10% of their old numbers. We are hopeful that they are now on the long road to recovery.

Gating a mine entrance

Some scientists have built artificial bat caves that can be cleaned of white-nose fungus. The yellow data logger in the photo above monitors temperature to help researchers learn whether bats will roost in the artificial caves.

A bat with fungus on its wing

SEVEN SICK SPECIES

BAT FACTS

White-nose syndrome has infected at least seven bat species so far. They are the little brown bat (*Myotis lucifugus*), big brown bat (*Eptesicus fuscus*), eastern small-footed bat (*Myotis leibii*), gray bat (*Myotis grisescens*), Indiana bat (*Myotis sodalis*), northern long-eared bat (*Myotis septentrionalis*), and tricolored bat (*Perimyotis subflavus*).

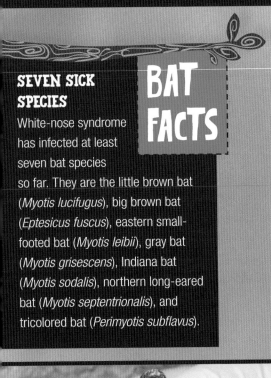

A northern long-eared bat with WNS

BAT CITIZEN: ALEXIS VALENTINE
CHECKING FOR BAT CHAT

Since the third grade, fourteen-year-old Alexis Valentine has been helping to monitor and research bats in and around the Great Smoky Mountains National Park at the border between North Carolina and Tennessee. She has held her own research permit with the park for several years. Using acoustic bat detectors at two sites, Alexis records bat echolocation calls on memory cards that she checks every seven to ten days. Using Sonobat computer software, she identifies which bat species are making the calls and how many calls are being recorded. Alexis is trying to determine if bat chat is changing due to white-nose syndrome. Her research is part of the larger effort aimed at learning more about how WNS is affecting bat populations. Alexis also competes in science fairs, regularly speaks to groups about bats and bat conservation, and has conducted fundraisers on behalf of bats. Her nickname is Batgirl and she is proud of it.

Alexis Valentine humanely trapping bats for tagging with a Tuttle trap

CHALLENGE: DISAPPEARING HOMES

Human activities are changing or destroying bat habitats. Forests and other bat-friendly environments have been destroyed and important roosting, maternity, and hibernation sites have been lost. The destruction of bat habitats also affects the insect populations that bats depend on for food.

SOLUTION: MAKING SPACE FOR BATS

If bats are to survive, then natural habitats and roosts must be protected. To give bats a helping hand, some communities and institutions have constructed large bat houses. The world's two largest are on the grounds of the University of Florida (UF) in the city of Gainesville. In 1987, the UF's historic Johnson Hall burned down, causing its resident bat colony to relocate to the concrete bleachers of a nearby football stadium. Urine and droppings from the bats created a nuisance, so in 1991 the university built a large bat house nearby to provide the bats with a new home. In 2009, part of the bat house collapsed due to the weight of the bats as well as wood rot from their urine and droppings. It was rebuilt and a second bat barn was constructed right next to it in 2010. Today, visitors can watch an estimated 300,000 Brazilian free-tailed bats (*Tadarida brasiliensis cynocephala*) emerge from these shelters at night.

Batty Ideas

TOWERING HOPES

A 50-year-old bat tower that burned down in 1979 may soon be rebuilt. The city of Temple Terrace, Florida, and the local preservation society plan to build a replica of the old wooden tower on the banks of the Hillsborough River. It will have room for up to 600,000 bats.

Kids helping build a bat box.

A Brazilian free-tailed bat

CHALLENGE: THAT MINE SHOULD BE MY MINE

Abandoned mines are incredibly important bat habitats because they often provide the same kind of protection and stable conditions as natural caves. Millions of bats are thought to be living in the estimated 300,000 abandoned mines in North America.

But there's a problem. Since abandoned mines can be unstable and dangerous if entered by humans, mining companies have sealed the entrances to a large number of them. They are bulldozed, plugged with concrete, or dynamited shut to prevent entry. When that happens, any bats living inside are trapped.

SOLUTION: PROTECTING UNDERGROUND HABITATS

Steel gates at cave and mine entrances are a simple way of protecting important underground habitats for bats. Gates are designed so that the gaps between the bars are too small for a person but big enough for bats to fly through. The gates are attached to the walls, floor, and ceiling of the entrance. Gate designs may change according to the species of bats in the cave or mine. But they all do the job of preventing bat disturbance and vandalism by humans.

This underground habitat is home to a colony of Wahlberg's epauletted fruit bats

Batty Ideas

CLOSE CALLS

Sometimes bat biologists manage to prevent the sealing of a mine entrance. In the 1990s, two mines scheduled for closure in Wisconsin were surveyed, revealing 600,000 bats of 4 species inside. The mines were kept open.

A gated cave entrance

Human vandals cause disturbance and make caves and mines less attractive to bats

CHALLENGE: NOISY NEIGHBORS

Hibernating bats can be extremely sensitive to temperature change and sound, especially high-pitched sound. In certain cases, just walking by can be enough to rouse hibernating bats. And since waking can take twenty to thirty minutes, it might seem like the bats are not bothered at all. If they wake too often, however, they use up all their critical fat reserves and starve to death before insect food becomes available in spring. Sound and temperature disturbances might also cause females to drop their pups to the floor below or, in some cases, make the whole colony abandon a roost. If that happens at multiple sites, then bat populations can plummet.

SOLUTION: DO NOT DISTURB

An easy way to help protect bats is to prevent disturbance, especially in maternity colonies or hibernacula. Many caves and mines have already been gated or fenced for this reason, and more will be closed to human entry in the future. Many amateur cavers who explore caves for fun now try to avoid disturbing bats. The "don't disturb bats" message seems to be reaching members of the public as well. There is still a long way to go, but the fight to prevent bat disturbance is moving people in the right direction.

Batty Ideas

ROAD HAZARD

New roads can destroy or break up vital bat habitat, and cars can cause noise, light, and air pollution. Moving vehicles may also hit and kill bats. On the positive side, some road bridges provide good roosting sites for bats, and some street lighting attracts insects for bats to eat. In a few cases, underpasses have been built where bat flyways cross roads, allowing bats to fly safely underneath.

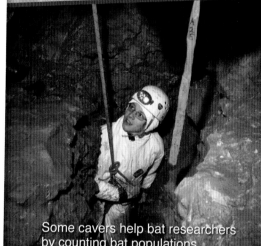

Some cavers help bat researchers by counting bat populations

ATTENTION!
CAVE ACCESS BY PERMIT ONLY

Permits may be obtained at the Entrance Station or Visitor Center

Mexican free-tailed bats in flight

CHALLENGE: TWISTING TURBINE TERROR

Wind turbines provide green energy but kill large numbers of bats each year. Turbines can be up to 262 feet (80 meters) tall or more, with massive rotating blades. The high-speed moving blades create low-pressure zones in the air around them. When bats fly into that zone, their lungs collapse. Bat Conservation International estimates that during the past 13 years, more than 2 million bats have been killed by wind turbines in North America alone.

SOLUTIONS TO TURBINE TERROR

Simple changes, such as turning wind turbines off at night or during low wind conditions in the summer and fall, can save a lot of bats without losing much power generation. And experts are now working on turbine designs and placements that will reduce the danger to bats and birds. Other promising developments that may help bats avoid turbines include ultrasonic "boom boxes" that send out constant high-pitched sounds (which jam bats' sonar) and ultraviolet light (to which many bats are sensitive). With so many people now working on this issue, new strategies for protecting bats from wind turbines are sure to emerge.

Wind turbines

BAT CITIZEN: CAMRYN PETTENGER-WILLEY
SEARCHING FOR SOLUTIONS

When she heard from her mother that bats were dying because of rotating wind turbine blades, thirteen-year-old Camryn Pettenger-Willey decided to look into the problem and figure out a solution. After consulting with a number of wind energy experts and scientists at Bat Conservation International, she learned that several devices were being developed to use sound to keep bats away from turbines. Camryn wondered if the bats could hear them and whether the position of the deterrent devices on the turbines made them more or less effective. She designed an experiment using regular fans and deer whistles, taking sound readings at several points around the fan. She discovered that the sound was strongest when it came from the nacelle, or center, of a fan, rather than from the blades. This finding could help determine the best place to position sound deterrents on wind turbines. Camryn's project was a semi-finalist in the Broadcom MASTERS program, meaning her project was one of the top 300 in the United States.

BAT FACTS

BATS NEED NIGHT, NOT LIGHT
Light pollution is another human-made disturbance for bats. Too much light can disrupt nighttime hunting patterns and, if it reduces the amount of food acquired by mothers, can even cause pups to go hungry. Whenever humans build in bat habitats, the effects of light pollution should be carefully considered.

BAT! SQUAD!

Batty Ideas

BATS IN YOUR OWN NEIGHBORHOOD

Organized bat walks that teach people about why bats are important are now very popular. Small groups of people follow a guide on an outdoor walk to search for bats using a handheld acoustic bat detector. Many people are buying their own detectors so they can search for bats in their gardens and neighborhoods.

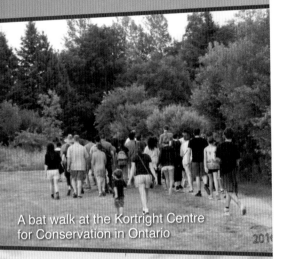
A bat walk at the Kortright Centre for Conservation in Ontario

A tourist at Bracken Cave

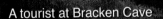

CHALLENGE: HUMANS THREATEN BATS

Millions of bats have been killed for human consumption in Asia, Africa, and on some Pacific islands. In many areas, fruit bats are also killed because they are considered pests that eat commercial fruit crops, while other kinds of bats are killed just because people misunderstand and are afraid of them.

SOLUTION: BAT TOURISM AND BAT WATCHING

Learning to understand and appreciate bats is an important step toward saving them. Increasingly, people are satisfying their curiosity about bats and seeing them in a new way by watching them in the wild. The most famous locations are the Congress Avenue Bridge and Bracken Cave in Texas. Elsewhere in the United States, people can observe large numbers of bats at Sauta Cave in Alabama, Orient Mine in Colorado, and Carlsbad Caverns National Park in New Mexico. Internationally, Monfort Bat Cave in the Philippines, the Battambang Bat Caves in Cambodia, Deer Cave and Dark Cave in Malaysia, Spandau Citadel in Germany, and Bat Island and the city of Cairns in Australia also provide outstanding bat-watching opportunities.

Carlsbad Caverns

BEING A FRIEND TO BATS

BAT-FRIENDLY HOMES

Sometimes bats enter buildings through tiny holes or gaps that lead into attics, basements, or spaces between walls. People often want them removed, but if pups are present, the bats should be left alone until the pups have weaned and both females and pups have left for the season. Hibernating bats should be left alone until after they wake up in the spring. If bats are roosting on the outside of a building, it's usually best to just leave them alone.

In the past, bats in buildings were often trapped and killed or their roosts were fumigated (filled with poisonous smoke). Sometimes they would just be sealed inside and left. These methods are cruel and unnecessary.

Today, there are humane ways of removing bats, including exclusion tubes that allow bats to leave a building from key entry points, but not re-enter. Once exclusion tubes are set up, other entry points can be sealed. People should avoid removal methods that involve plastic sheeting, materials with sharp edges, chemicals, traps, flexible bird netting, and sticky materials that can trap or injure bats.

Batty Ideas

BAT-FRIENDLY GARDENS

Trees, bushes, and other vegetation can attract insects for bats to eat and also provide good roost sites. Large snags (dead trees that are still standing) with peeling bark are especially good for tree-roosting bats. Fruit trees and flower gardens in warmer climates may entice both fruit and pollinating bats, while pools and ponds can provide bats with drinking water. Keep bright light and loud noise away from your garden to make it more bat friendly.

A disease called *histoplasmosis* is caused by breathing in spores from a fungus in some bird and bat guano (droppings). Anyone cleaning up large piles of guano should wear protective clothing and a special face mask. With some simple precautions, the chances of contracting histoplasmosis are very small.

This big brown bat was caught in a house

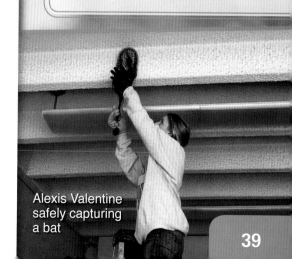

Alexis Valentine safely capturing a bat

BAT CITIZEN: CALVIN CARPENTER
BAT MAPPING

Batty Ideas

CITIZEN BAT SCIENTISTS

Many research projects involve volunteers who help gather information about bats. Becoming a citizen scientist can be as easy as calling your local or regional bat group or fish and wildlife agency to find out what projects need help. Some organizations that welcome volunteers include the Neighbourhood Bat Watch in Canada, the Wisconsin Bat Program, and the Bat Conservation Trust in England.

After becoming interested in bats in the fourth grade, Calvin Carpenter learned about the threat of WNS. He wondered if the Mexican free-tailed bats in his area of Texas could become infected by the fungus. With some research, Calvin found that tricolored bats in Arkansas, about 500 miles (806 kilometers) away, were the closest bats affected with WNS. With his mother Penny's help, Calvin used special mapping software to see if the summer habitat ranges of the two bat species overlapped. They didn't, so Calvin concluded that the fungus was not likely to spread to his area. His maps won first prize in a regional science competition. More recently, Calvin has been conducting winter surveys of the availability of bat food around several high-priority caves in Texas. He is focusing on a local bat species, the cave myotis (*Myotis velifer*), and the moths that are its favorite prey.

BAT CITIZENS: ELEANOR & SAMSON DAVIS

SAVE THE BATS

During a family holiday in Australia, five-year-old Eleanor and four-year-old Samson were able to see bats leaving their roosts each night to forage for food. Bats soon became a popular family discussion topic. When they returned home, Eleanor and Samson encountered bats during a presentation at the American Museum of Natural History. Samson liked that bats eat mosquitoes. Eleanor learned about white-nose syndrome (WNS). She told everyone she could about how important bats are, but Eleanor wanted to help bats even more by setting up a lemonade stand to raise funds. Her mom suggested making it a hot chocolate stand instead because the weather in New York was quite cold. So hot chocolate it was. Eleanor and Samson raised the impressive sum of $104, which they donated to the Organization for Bat Conservation.

Batty Ideas

BAT HABITATS ARE BEING PROTECTED

People and governments around the world are working to save bat habitats. In Europe, Poland's Nietoperek Bat Nature Reserve—a system of abandoned underground World War II bunkers that thousands of bats call home—was established in 1980. Since the 1990s, the Vincent Wildlife Trust in England has acquired and protected more than forty bat roosting sites. In 2010, Scotland's first-ever bat reserve was established. These efforts show that protecting habitat helps bats. A 2014 European Environment Agency report on bat populations reveals that between 1993 and 2011, the numbers of some bat species in Europe increased by more than 40%.

BAT FACTS

Sodalis Nature Preserve

A tourist at Bracken Cave

PEOPLE ARE CELEBRATING BATS

Every summer, tens of thousands of people gather on the Congress Avenue Bridge in Austin, Texas, for the annual Bat Fest, a celebration of the estimated 1.5–2 million bats that live under the bridge. The event features live music, food, arts and crafts, and children's bat-themed events.

In 2016, Hannibal, Missouri, held its first-ever BatFest to celebrate the approximately 170,000 endangered Indiana bats (*Myotis sodalis*), one third of the species' entire known population, living in the near-by Sodalis Nature Preserve. The bats live in limestone mines that were closed in the 1960s. Visitors can follow woodland trails right up to the gated mine entrances and watch the bats emerge at dusk or return at dawn.

The Great Lakes Bat Festival—a series of events in several cities—is conducted by the Organization for Bat Conservation. And throughout Europe and other parts of the world, hundreds of bat walks, exhibitions, and public awareness events take place on International Bat Night in late August.

Bat watchers on the Congress Avenue Bridge in Austin, Texas

SOMETIMES BATS NEED A HELPING HAND

Wildlife rescue organizations are saving bats in need. Every year, the Toronto Wildlife Centre (TWC) helps thousands of animals, including injured, sick, and starving bats.

In 2014, the TWC took in 35 bats that had been woken from hibernation in the middle of winter. They were weak, vulnerable, and had used up most of their fat reserves. The TWC hand-fed the bats 1,600 mealworms a day, and 33 of them survived.

DO BATS HAVE A FUTURE?

While there are many positive developments for bats, they are still in trouble and need our help. I hope you decide to become a bat friend and advocate—a Bat Citizen. Just think about how you can help and then get to it. If enough of us speak up for bats, they will be with us for a very long time. The world would be a poorer place without bats.

A Malayan flying fox

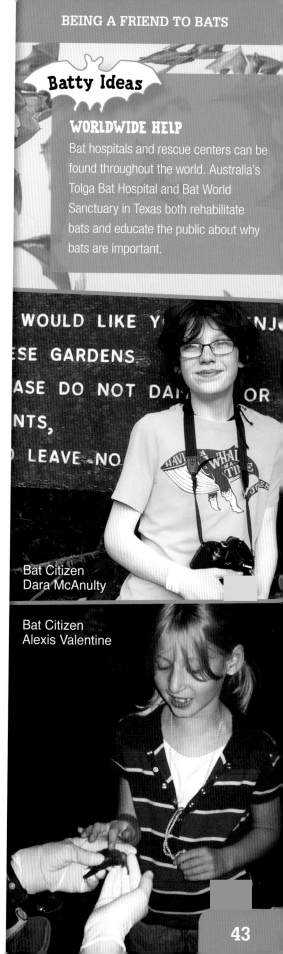

Batty Ideas

WORLDWIDE HELP

Bat hospitals and rescue centers can be found throughout the world. Australia's Tolga Bat Hospital and Bat World Sanctuary in Texas both rehabilitate bats and educate the public about why bats are important.

Bat Citizen
Dara McAnulty

Bat Citizen
Alexis Valentine

43

14 WAYS YOU CAN HELP BATS

Bat boxes on a tree

Bat Citizen Truth Muller

1. Learn as much as you can about bat biology, behavior, and conservation.

2. Make your own home and garden bat friendly.

3. Make your school yard or community bat friendly by planting bat-friendly vegetation, making sure that large trees and snags are not cut down, erecting bat boxes, and making sure there are safe sources of water for bats to drink.

4. Do a school project to help dispel the myths about bats and to encourage others to protect them. Better yet, start a school or community bat festival.

5. If you find bats in your home, school, or business, don't harass them or seal their entry holes. Mothers with dependent pups or hibernating bats might be present. There are humane ways of removing bats from buildings. Get expert advice from a bat rescue or conservation group.

6. Tell your community leaders and elected representatives about bats and why they are important.

7. Write a letter to the editor of your local newspaper to tell everyone why we need bats.

8. Support or get involved in efforts to protect natural habitats in your own town, city, or region. Look for groups that already have local projects that you can help out with.

9. Don't disturb bats. Stay out of caves, mines, tunnels, culverts, old buildings, and other areas where there are bats.

10. Never keep a bat as a pet. If you see bats being sold as pets, notify a bat rescue group or conservation organization.

11. Become a citizen bat scientist by volunteering to help out with a local bat count or offer your time to a bat research project.

12. Sponsor or adopt a bat and support the work of bat hospitals and rescues.

13. Raise funds for a bat conservation organization that works to protect both above-ground and below-ground bat habitats.

14. Participate in bat walks or bat tours.

ORGANIZATIONS THAT HELP BATS

African Bat Conservation
www.africanbatconservation.org

Australasian Bat Society
www.ausbats.org.au

Bat Conservation India Trust
www.batconservationindia.org

Bat Conservation International
www.batcon.org

Bat Conservation Trust
www.bats.org.uk

Bat World Sanctuary
https://batworld.org

Bats Northwest (Bat House Central)
www.batsnorthwest.org/bat_house_central.html

Buddies for Bats
www.facebook.com/LilBrownBat/

Community Bat Programs of BC
www.bcbats.ca

Florida Bat Conservancy
www.floridabats.org
Lubee Bat Conservancy
www.lubee.org

Neighbourhood Bat Watch
batwatch.ca

North American Bat Conservation Alliance
www.batconservationalliance.org

Organization for Bat Conservation
www.batconservation.org

The Save Lucy Campaign
www.savelucythebat.org

Sticks and Stones Rescue
www.sticksandstonesrescue.org

Tolga Bat Hospital
www.tolgabathospital.org

Toronto Wildlife Centre
www.torontowildlifecenter.com

White-Nose Syndrome.org
www.whitenosesyndrome.org

Egyptian fruit bats in flight

GLOSSARY

acoustic bat detector
a device that converts bat sounds into a form humans can see or hear

adaptation
a change or alteration to an organism that makes the organism better able to survive in its environment

bat box
a special wooden shelter for bats built by humans

bat census
an organized count or survey of bat populations

carnivorous
meat-eating

colony
a group that includes many members of the same species living together

conservation
preserving or protecting natural environments and wildlife

echolocation
a process that many bats use to map their surroundings by producing high-frequency sounds and listening to their echoes as they bounce off objects

foraging
seeking food

frugivorous
fruit-eating

hibernaculum, hibernacula (pl.)
a cool, moist, sheltered place where bats hibernate during the winter

hibernation
a resting state in which bats' body processes slow, letting them save energy and sleep through the winter

insectivorous
insect-eating

mammal
a warm-blooded animal that has hair and nurses its young with milk from mammary glands

maternity roost
a sheltered place where female bats gather to bear and raise their young

megabat
a suborder of bats that includes Old World fruit bats and flying foxes

microbat
a suborder of bats that includes mostly insect-eating bats that use echolocation

nectarivorous
nectar-eating

pollinator
an insect, bird, bat, or other animal that transfers pollen from one flower to another

predator
an animal or species that lives by feeding on other creatures

prey
an animal or species that is eaten by other creatures

rehabilitation
the process of making a sick or injured creature healthy enough for release back into the wild

roost
a sheltered place where bats rest during the day

sanguinivorous
blood-eating

ultrasonic
high-pitched sounds that humans cannot hear

uropatagium
A membrane that stretches between the legs of bats

white-nose syndrome
a new disease of hibernating bats in North America that often grows a white fungus ring on the noses of infected individuals

wind turbine
a structure with large blades turned by the wind to generate electrical energy

wingspan
when a pair of wings is fully outstretched, the distance from one wingtip to the other

A Davis's round-eared bat

INDEX

PHOTO CREDITS